PRINCEWILL LAGANG

Forging an Equal Partnership

First published by PRINCEWILL LAGANG 2023

Copyright © 2023 by Princewill Lagang

All rights reserved. No part of this publication may be reproduced, stored or transmitted in any form or by any means, electronic, mechanical, photocopying, recording, scanning, or otherwise without written permission from the publisher. It is illegal to copy this book, post it to a website, or distribute it by any other means without permission.

Princewill Lagang asserts the moral right to be identified as the author of this work.

First edition

This book was professionally typeset on Reedsy.
Find out more at reedsy.com

Contents

1. Introduction — 1
2. The Evolving Landscape of Relationships — 4
3. Shared Decision-Making — 7
4. Equitable Division of Household Responsibilities — 10
5. Navigating Career and Family Balance — 13
6. Financial Equality and Transparency — 16
7. Emotional Labor and Communication — 19
8. Parenting as Partners — 22
9. Respecting Individual Needs and Identities — 25
10. Conflict Resolution and Collaboration — 28
11. Celebrating Achievements and Milestones — 31
12. Cultivating an Ongoing Partnership — 34

1

Introduction

In a world where relationships and partnerships play a pivotal role in our lives, the pursuit of a balanced and equal partnership has never been more significant. This book delves into the intricacies of fostering such relationships, where both individuals can thrive in harmony and mutual understanding. By examining the core values of shared responsibilities, respect, and collaboration, we aim to provide a comprehensive guide to building relationships that stand the test of time.

The Need for Balance and Equality

In our modern society, the dynamics of partnerships have evolved considerably. No longer confined by traditional gender roles or societal norms, individuals now seek relationships built on shared aspirations, goals, and responsibilities. The pursuit of personal fulfillment and happiness within partnerships has shifted the focus towards achieving a balanced and equal dynamic. It is within this context that we embark on a journey to explore the key elements that contribute to the creation of such partnerships.

Shared Responsibilities: A Foundation for Growth

One of the fundamental pillars of a successful and enduring partnership is the concept of shared responsibilities. Gone are the days when roles were strictly defined by gender or external expectations. Instead, couples now find themselves striving for an equitable distribution of tasks and obligations. This chapter will delve into the significance of sharing responsibilities within a partnership, not only as a means to lighten the burden but also as a way to strengthen the bond between individuals. Real-life examples and practical strategies will be discussed to illustrate how embracing shared responsibilities can lead to a more fulfilling and harmonious partnership.

Respect: The Bedrock of Connection

Respect serves as the bedrock upon which a balanced and equal partnership is built. Without mutual respect, any relationship is susceptible to deterioration. This section will delve into the various facets of respect, from valuing each other's opinions and boundaries to appreciating individual differences. By fostering an environment of respect, partners can create a safe space where open communication and vulnerability thrive. Through anecdotes and insights, we will explore how cultivating respect can fortify the foundation of a lasting partnership.

The Power of Collaboration

Collaboration is the synergy that emerges when two individuals pool their strengths, skills, and perspectives to achieve shared goals. This chapter will emphasize the transformative potential of collaboration within a partnership. By approaching challenges and triumphs as a united front, couples can create a momentum that propels them forward. We will delve into effective communication techniques, active listening, and the art of compromise, all of which contribute to a partnership characterized by collaboration and teamwork.

In the pages that follow, we will journey through the intricacies of partnership,

INTRODUCTION

drawing from psychological insights, real-world experiences, and expert advice. By examining the principles of shared responsibilities, respect, and collaboration, we hope to provide you with a comprehensive toolkit for cultivating a relationship that thrives on balance and equality. As we embark on this exploration, remember that the path to a harmonious partnership is uniquely yours to navigate, and this book is here to guide and support you every step of the way.

2

The Evolving Landscape of Relationships

In recent decades, the landscape of relationships has undergone a profound transformation. Societal norms and expectations that once dictated rigid roles within partnerships have given way to a more fluid and egalitarian approach. This chapter explores the fascinating journey of this evolution, from traditional expectations to the modern emphasis on equal roles and shared responsibilities within relationships.

Shifting Societal Norms

The traditional model of relationships was often characterized by distinct gender roles, with men as primary breadwinners and women as homemakers. However, as societies began to challenge and redefine these norms, a shift occurred in the way partnerships were perceived. The liberation movements of the 20th century sparked discussions about equality and women's rights, paving the way for a broader reconsideration of the dynamics within relationships. This section delves into the historical context that set the stage for a departure from traditional norms.

Redefining Partnership Dynamics

As societies recognized the importance of equal rights and opportunities, the dynamics of relationships started to transform. Partnerships evolved from being solely based on economic stability and familial duties to becoming platforms for mutual growth, companionship, and shared aspirations. The rise of dual-income households and the increasing emphasis on personal fulfillment highlighted the need for both partners to contribute to various aspects of the partnership. This chapter explores how these changes have paved the way for a more balanced distribution of roles and responsibilities within relationships.

Equal Roles, Shared Responsibilities

In the modern landscape of relationships, equality has become a cornerstone. Partners now seek a balance where both individuals contribute to decision-making, household chores, and the raising of children. This section delves into the benefits of embracing equal roles and shared responsibilities, not only in terms of fostering a healthier partnership but also in modeling positive behaviors for future generations. We will discuss how open communication and collaboration play crucial roles in creating a partnership where each person's strengths are recognized and valued.

Navigating Challenges

While the shift toward equal roles and shared responsibilities is a positive one, it's not without its challenges. This chapter will address potential obstacles that couples may face, such as societal pressures, internalized beliefs, and external judgments. Strategies for overcoming these challenges will be explored, including effective communication, setting boundaries, and seeking support when needed. By acknowledging the potential roadblocks, partners can navigate them with resilience and maintain the integrity of their balanced partnership.

As we delve into the evolving landscape of relationships, it's clear that the traditional notions of partnership have given way to a more inclusive, balanced, and dynamic approach. By embracing equal roles and shared responsibilities, individuals are paving the way for relationships that are built on respect, collaboration, and mutual growth. In the chapters that follow, we will continue to explore practical strategies and insights to help you navigate this evolving landscape and create a partnership that stands the test of time.

3

Shared Decision-Making

In a balanced and equal partnership, shared decision-making emerges as a vital component that reflects the respect and collaboration between partners. This chapter delves into the profound significance of involving both individuals in the decision-making process and provides practical strategies for making choices collaboratively and inclusively.

The Importance of Shared Decision-Making

Gone are the days when decisions were made unilaterally within relationships. Shared decision-making recognizes the unique perspectives, values, and aspirations of each partner. It acknowledges that both individuals contribute to the partnership's overall vision and deserve a voice in shaping its direction. This section explores the profound impact of shared decision-making on building trust, mutual understanding, and a sense of ownership within the partnership.

Fostering Open Communication

Central to shared decision-making is open and effective communication.

Partners must feel comfortable expressing their thoughts, concerns, and desires without fear of judgment. This chapter highlights the significance of active listening, empathy, and validation in creating an environment where both individuals can freely share their perspectives. We'll discuss techniques for cultivating open communication, such as regular check-ins, creating a safe space for discussions, and practicing patience when differences arise.

Collaborative Strategies for Decision-Making

Making decisions collaboratively involves finding common ground and combining both partners' insights to arrive at choices that honor both perspectives. This section delves into various strategies that encourage collaborative decision-making, including brainstorming sessions, compromise, and consensus building. Real-life examples will illustrate how couples can work together to identify solutions that align with their shared goals and values.

Inclusivity in Decision-Making

Inclusivity within decision-making extends beyond the immediate partnership. It involves recognizing the impact of choices on individuals and communities outside the relationship. This chapter explores the importance of considering external factors, seeking diverse perspectives, and making choices that align with ethical and moral principles. By broadening the scope of decision-making to encompass a larger context, partners can contribute positively to their broader surroundings.

Navigating Differences

Shared decision-making doesn't eliminate the potential for differences in opinion. Instead, it equips partners with tools to navigate these differences constructively. This section will address strategies for managing disagreements, such as active problem-solving, reframing issues, and practicing empathy. By approaching disagreements as opportunities for growth, couples can transform challenges into catalysts for deeper understanding and connection.

As we delve into the art of shared decision-making, it becomes clear that this practice is a reflection of a partnership's commitment to mutual respect, active collaboration, and individual growth. By embracing inclusive communication and collaborative strategies, partners can ensure that their decisions reflect the shared values and aspirations that form the foundation of their relationship. In the chapters ahead, we'll continue to explore avenues for building a partnership that thrives on shared decision-making, fostering a sense of unity and purpose that strengthens over time.

4

Equitable Division of Household Responsibilities

In the pursuit of a balanced and equal partnership, the equitable division of household responsibilities emerges as a critical aspect of creating harmony and shared fulfillment. This chapter addresses the challenges associated with household chores and responsibilities and offers practical techniques for distributing tasks fairly and according to each partner's strengths.

Recognizing the Challenges

Household responsibilities, from cleaning to cooking to managing finances, can sometimes become sources of tension within a relationship. Historically, these tasks were often assigned based on gender roles, leading to an uneven burden on one partner. This section explores the challenges that arise when responsibilities are not evenly shared and highlights the importance of addressing these challenges to create a thriving partnership.

The Power of Communication

Effective communication lies at the heart of achieving an equitable division of household responsibilities. Partners must openly discuss their expectations, preferences, and limitations when it comes to tasks. This chapter emphasizes the significance of setting clear boundaries, expressing needs, and actively listening to each other's perspectives. By fostering an environment where communication flows freely, partners can work together to design a fair and effective system for managing household responsibilities.

Playing to Strengths

Equitable division doesn't necessarily mean splitting each task exactly in half. Instead, partners can leverage their individual strengths and preferences to create a system that plays to each person's abilities. This section explores the concept of complementary strengths, where tasks are assigned based on who is better suited for them. From cooking to home repairs, understanding and utilizing each partner's strengths can result in a more efficient and enjoyable division of responsibilities.

Creating a Shared System

Implementing a shared system for household responsibilities requires collaboration and compromise. Partners must discuss and agree on the allocation of tasks, taking into account work schedules, personal preferences, and the importance of balancing individual leisure time. This chapter delves into strategies for creating a shared system, such as designing chore charts, rotating responsibilities, and establishing regular check-ins to assess the effectiveness of the arrangement.

Overcoming Traditional Expectations

Overcoming deeply ingrained traditional expectations is essential for achieving an equitable division of responsibilities. Societal norms can sometimes influence how partners perceive their roles within the home. This section addresses the importance of challenging these norms and embracing a new mindset that values shared contributions and individual growth. By breaking free from antiquated expectations, couples can pave the way for a partnership that thrives on equality and mutual respect.

As we navigate the complexities of household responsibilities, it becomes evident that an equitable division is not just about tasks but about nurturing a relationship that values each partner's contributions and aspirations. By communicating openly, capitalizing on strengths, and designing a system that honors both individuals, couples can create a household environment that reflects the essence of their balanced and equal partnership. The chapters ahead will continue to explore practical strategies and insights to guide you on this journey of building a relationship grounded in shared responsibilities and mutual growth.

5

Navigating Career and Family Balance

In the modern landscape of partnerships, the delicate balance between professional aspirations and family life has become a significant consideration. This chapter delves into the complexities of managing careers and family responsibilities while maintaining a sense of equality and mutual support. It provides insights into how partners can navigate this balance, fostering an environment where both career goals and parental responsibilities can flourish.

Understanding the Dual Role

Balancing a career with family responsibilities requires recognizing the dual role that partners play. They are not just individuals pursuing professional success but also integral members of a family unit. This section explores the challenges that can arise when trying to juggle these roles and highlights the importance of open communication in managing expectations and finding alignment between individual aspirations and family needs.

Supporting Career Aspirations

In a balanced partnership, both individuals' career aspirations should be valued and supported. This chapter delves into strategies for fostering an environment that encourages the pursuit of professional growth. Partners can offer each other encouragement, share insights, and create opportunities for skill development. By viewing each other's career goals as shared endeavors, couples can strengthen their bond and create a foundation for mutual success.

Shared Parental Responsibilities

Parental responsibilities present another layer of complexity in the career and family balance. Partners must collaborate to ensure that child-rearing duties are shared fairly and equitably. This section discusses the importance of acknowledging both partners' contributions to parenting, from caregiving tasks to decision-making. By creating a plan that considers each person's strengths and commitments, couples can navigate the demands of parenthood while maintaining their own sense of identity and fulfillment.

Flexible Work-Life Integration

The boundaries between work and personal life are becoming increasingly fluid, particularly with the rise of remote work and flexible schedules. This chapter explores how partners can navigate the integration of work and family life, allowing for greater flexibility in managing both. Strategies such as setting boundaries, designing shared calendars, and embracing the concept of work-life integration can help partners create a sustainable rhythm that promotes harmony between professional and familial responsibilities.

Prioritizing Self-Care

Amidst the demands of career and family, self-care often takes a back seat. However, maintaining individual well-being is crucial for both partners to thrive in their respective roles. This section addresses the significance of prioritizing self-care and offers suggestions for carving out time for relaxation, hobbies, and personal growth. Partners can encourage each other to prioritize self-care, leading to improved mental and emotional well-being.

As we navigate the intricate balance between career aspirations and family responsibilities, it becomes evident that a thriving partnership is one where both individuals feel supported, valued, and understood. By fostering an environment of mutual encouragement, effective communication, and shared responsibilities, couples can navigate the complexities of modern life while preserving the foundation of equality and harmony within their relationship. The chapters that follow will continue to provide practical insights and guidance to assist you in creating a partnership that flourishes both in your professional pursuits and in your roles as parents.

6

Financial Equality and Transparency

In a balanced and equal partnership, financial matters hold significant weight. Financial transparency and equality not only provide a strong foundation for a harmonious relationship but also reflect the mutual trust and collaboration between partners. This chapter delves into the importance of open communication about money matters and offers strategies for managing finances as a team, making joint decisions, and achieving financial equality.

The Significance of Financial Transparency

Money can be a source of both joy and stress within a partnership. Financial transparency, where partners openly share their financial situations, goals, and concerns, is essential for building trust and understanding. This section explores how financial transparency fosters a sense of unity and shared responsibility, allowing partners to work together towards common financial objectives.

Creating a Joint Financial Vision

FINANCIAL EQUALITY AND TRANSPARENCY

To ensure financial equality and success, partners must create a joint financial vision. This chapter discusses the importance of setting shared financial goals, such as savings targets, investments, and long-term plans. Partners can collaborate to outline their priorities and aspirations, laying the groundwork for a united approach to managing money.

Managing Money as a Team

Treating finances as a collaborative effort rather than an individual responsibility is key to achieving financial equality. This section delves into practical strategies for managing money as a team, including creating a joint bank account, allocating funds for shared expenses, and setting a budget that aligns with both partners' values. By working together to track expenses and monitor progress, couples can ensure that their financial decisions reflect their shared vision.

Making Joint Financial Decisions

Joint financial decisions require effective communication and compromise. This chapter delves into techniques for making financial choices together, from major purchases to investment decisions. Partners must be willing to engage in open discussions, actively listen to each other's perspectives, and find solutions that honor both individuals' goals and preferences.

Equity in Financial Contributions

Financial equality goes beyond splitting bills; it involves recognizing and valuing each partner's contributions, whether monetary or non-monetary. This section addresses strategies for maintaining equity in financial contributions, particularly in cases where there might be income disparities or career changes. Partners can establish a system that ensures both individuals feel empowered and respected in their financial roles.

Emergency Planning and Long-Term Security

Planning for emergencies and securing a stable future are integral to financial equality. This chapter explores the importance of creating emergency funds, discussing insurance coverage, and setting long-term financial goals, such as retirement planning. Partners can collaborate to ensure that they are both prepared for unexpected challenges and positioned for sustained financial well-being.

As we navigate the realm of financial matters within a partnership, it becomes clear that financial transparency and equality are cornerstones of a strong and thriving relationship. By openly discussing money matters, working together to create shared financial goals, and making joint decisions, couples can foster an environment of trust, collaboration, and mutual respect. The following chapters will continue to provide insights and guidance to assist you in building a relationship that flourishes both personally and financially.

7

Emotional Labor and Communication

In the intricate web of a partnership, emotional labor stands as a cornerstone that can greatly influence the quality of the relationship. This chapter delves into the concept of emotional labor and explores the importance of sharing emotional support, practicing active listening, and fostering a deep understanding to create a balanced and equal partnership.

Understanding Emotional Labor

Emotional labor encompasses the effort invested in managing one's own emotions, responding to the emotions of others, and maintaining the emotional well-being of the relationship. This section explores the significance of recognizing and valuing emotional labor within a partnership. It also emphasizes that sharing this labor is essential for building a foundation of mutual support and understanding.

Sharing Emotional Support

A balanced partnership requires both individuals to share the responsibility of providing emotional support. This chapter discusses strategies for offering empathy, reassurance, and encouragement to each other during times of joy, stress, and vulnerability. Partners can create an environment where emotional expression is welcomed and validated, strengthening the bond between them.

Practicing Active Listening

Active listening is a powerful tool in fostering effective communication and mutual understanding. This section delves into the art of active listening, where partners give each other their full attention, show empathy, and seek to understand without judgment. By practicing active listening, couples can create a space where both individuals feel heard and valued, leading to improved emotional connection.

Fostering Deep Understanding

Building a partnership based on deep understanding involves recognizing each other's needs, preferences, and emotional triggers. This chapter explores the importance of exploring each other's perspectives, beliefs, and experiences. By delving into each other's emotional worlds, partners can cultivate a sense of compassion and empathy that forms the bedrock of a balanced relationship.

Balancing Emotional Labor

Balancing emotional labor involves being mindful of each partner's emotional capacity and boundaries. This section addresses the importance of open communication about emotional needs and stressors. Partners can collaborate to find strategies for managing emotional labor in a way that supports both individuals' well-being.

Nurturing Emotional Intimacy

Emotional intimacy is a profound aspect of a balanced partnership. This chapter discusses the significance of cultivating emotional intimacy through vulnerable conversations, shared experiences, and mutual vulnerability. By sharing their inner thoughts and feelings, partners can deepen their connection and build a relationship that thrives on emotional closeness.

As we explore the realm of emotional labor and communication, it becomes evident that nurturing emotional support, active listening, and understanding are crucial elements of building a partnership characterized by equality and mutual growth. By valuing and sharing emotional labor, partners can create a space where both individuals feel seen, heard, and cherished, enriching the fabric of their relationship. The forthcoming chapters will continue to provide insights and guidance to help you navigate the intricacies of a partnership rooted in emotional connection and understanding.

8

Parenting as Partners

Parenting is a journey that profoundly impacts a partnership, shaping its dynamics and values. Co-parenting, where both partners share the responsibilities and joys of raising children, is essential for forging an equal partnership that thrives on collaboration and shared growth. This chapter delves into the role of co-parenting in creating an equal partnership and offers insights into balancing parental roles and promoting shared parenting values.

The Importance of Co-Parenting

Co-parenting is more than just sharing childcare duties; it's about working together as a team to raise children with love, respect, and shared values. This section explores the significance of co-parenting in building a balanced partnership. It emphasizes the positive impact of both partners being actively engaged in parenting, contributing to their children's well-being, and fostering a sense of unity in the family.

Balancing Parental Roles

In an equal partnership, parental roles should be balanced to reflect the unique strengths and contributions of both partners. This chapter delves into strategies for distributing parenting responsibilities fairly, from diaper changes to school activities. By acknowledging and valuing each partner's role, couples can ensure that the demands of parenting do not disrupt the equilibrium of their partnership.

Promoting Shared Parenting Values

Shared parenting values are the foundation upon which co-parenting is built. This section discusses the importance of aligning on key parenting principles, such as discipline, communication, and emotional support. Partners can engage in open discussions to explore their parenting values, allowing them to present a united front and provide consistent guidance to their children.

Effective Communication in Co-Parenting

Effective communication is at the heart of successful co-parenting. This chapter explores the role of communication in managing parenting decisions, discussing challenges, and celebrating successes. Partners must openly express their perspectives, actively listen, and find compromises that reflect the best interests of their children and the well-being of their partnership.

Modeling Equality for Children

Co-parenting as partners not only benefits the relationship but also serves as a powerful model for children. This section addresses the significance of modeling equality, mutual respect, and collaboration in parenting. By demonstrating these values in their co-parenting efforts, partners can impart valuable lessons to their children about healthy relationships and gender equality.

Nurturing Quality Time as a Family

Amidst the demands of co-parenting, carving out quality family time becomes essential. This chapter discusses the importance of creating meaningful experiences together, fostering emotional connections, and ensuring that children feel loved and supported. Partners can work together to design family rituals and traditions that strengthen their bond and create lasting memories.

As we navigate the realm of co-parenting and parenting as partners, it's clear that this journey is integral to creating an equal partnership that extends to all aspects of life. By valuing each other's roles, aligning on shared parenting values, and fostering effective communication, couples can build a family dynamic that reflects the principles of equality, collaboration, and mutual growth. The forthcoming chapters will continue to provide insights and guidance to help you navigate the complexities of co-parenting and create a partnership that flourishes in all realms.

9

Respecting Individual Needs and Identities

In the intricate dance of partnership, it's essential to honor and nurture each partner's individuality. Respecting individual needs and identities forms the cornerstone of a balanced and equal relationship. This chapter delves into the significance of maintaining personal individuality within a partnership and offers insights into supporting each other's personal growth, interests, and aspirations.

Embracing Individuality

While partnership brings people together, it's crucial to remember that each individual retains their unique needs, aspirations, and identity. This section explores the importance of allowing space for personal growth and maintaining a sense of self within the partnership. It highlights how embracing individuality enhances the partnership by bringing together two whole individuals who contribute their strengths and passions.

Supporting Personal Growth

A balanced partnership encourages and supports personal growth for both partners. This chapter discusses strategies for providing the necessary encouragement, resources, and space for each person to pursue their personal goals, whether they involve education, career advancement, or self-discovery. Partners can celebrate each other's achievements and provide a solid foundation from which personal aspirations can flourish.

Nurturing Interests and Passions

Partnerships thrive when each individual has the freedom to pursue their interests and passions. This section delves into the importance of fostering an environment where both partners can engage in activities that bring them joy and fulfillment. Partners can participate in each other's interests, create opportunities for shared experiences, and demonstrate genuine enthusiasm for each other's pursuits.

Encouraging Autonomy

Respecting individual needs and identities involves acknowledging that each partner has their own autonomy. This chapter addresses the importance of allowing each other to make decisions independently and having a sense of agency within the partnership. Partners can communicate openly about their desires and boundaries, fostering an environment where autonomy is cherished and respected.

Balancing Togetherness and Independence

Balancing togetherness with independence is a delicate art in a partnership. This section explores how partners can find a harmonious balance that allows for quality time together while also respecting the need for solitude and personal space. By communicating openly about their preferences and needs, couples can create a dynamic that supports both togetherness and individuality.

Fostering Mutual Support

Supporting individual needs and identities goes hand in hand with offering mutual encouragement and support. This chapter discusses the significance of being each other's cheerleaders, offering a shoulder to lean on during challenges, and celebrating personal milestones. Partners can create an environment where they feel secure in pursuing their individual journeys while knowing that they have a reliable source of emotional support.

As we explore the realm of respecting individual needs and identities, it's evident that this practice is foundational to creating a partnership that thrives on equality, understanding, and mutual growth. By valuing personal growth, interests, and autonomy, couples can foster a relationship where both individuals are free to explore their passions and evolve as individuals. The forthcoming chapters will continue to provide insights and guidance to help you navigate the intricacies of maintaining individuality within the context of a balanced partnership.

10

Conflict Resolution and Collaboration

Conflict is an inevitable aspect of any relationship, but it's how conflicts are approached and resolved that can significantly shape the nature of a partnership. In a balanced and equal relationship, conflicts are viewed as opportunities for growth, understanding, and strengthening the bond. This chapter addresses the importance of conflict resolution as a tool for collaboration and offers insights into navigating disagreements respectfully and finding compromise.

Conflict as a Catalyst for Growth

Conflicts, when approached with the right mindset, can serve as catalysts for personal growth and relationship development. This section explores the significance of viewing conflicts as opportunities to better understand each other's perspectives, values, and boundaries. By addressing conflicts openly and constructively, couples can deepen their connection and build a stronger foundation of trust and mutual respect.

Effective Communication in Conflict

CONFLICT RESOLUTION AND COLLABORATION

Effective communication is pivotal in resolving conflicts and fostering collaboration. This chapter delves into techniques for engaging in productive conversations during times of disagreement. Partners must express themselves honestly, practice active listening, and validate each other's feelings. By creating an environment where both individuals feel heard and understood, couples can prevent conflicts from escalating and work towards resolution.

Seeking Common Ground

In a balanced partnership, conflicts are approached with a shared goal of finding common ground and compromise. This section discusses the importance of focusing on the underlying issues rather than getting caught up in trivial disagreements. Partners can collaborate to identify shared interests, explore solutions, and arrive at resolutions that honor both individuals' needs.

Respecting Differences of Opinion

Respecting differences of opinion is crucial in conflict resolution. This chapter addresses the significance of valuing each other's perspectives, even when disagreements arise. Partners can engage in respectful discussions, acknowledge that different viewpoints are natural, and seek to find solutions that accommodate both individuals' preferences.

Practicing Empathy and Understanding

Empathy and understanding play a pivotal role in resolving conflicts collaboratively. This section explores the practice of putting oneself in the other person's shoes, recognizing their emotions, and considering their point of view. By approaching conflicts with empathy, couples can create an atmosphere where partners feel safe expressing themselves and finding common ground.

The Art of Compromise

Compromise is a cornerstone of conflict resolution within a partnership. This chapter discusses the importance of finding middle ground and making concessions to reach resolutions. Partners can engage in negotiations, explore creative solutions, and demonstrate a willingness to adjust their positions for the sake of maintaining harmony within the relationship.

As we delve into the realm of conflict resolution and collaboration, it becomes evident that these skills are integral to building a balanced and equal partnership. By approaching conflicts as opportunities for growth, valuing effective communication, and seeking common ground, couples can transform disagreements into stepping stones towards deeper understanding and mutual respect. The forthcoming chapters will continue to provide insights and guidance to help you navigate conflicts constructively and create a relationship that flourishes through collaboration and resolution.

11

Celebrating Achievements and Milestones

In a balanced and equal partnership, celebrating successes and achievements together serves as a powerful way to reinforce the foundation of mutual support and shared joy. This chapter delves into the significance of acknowledging each other's accomplishments and offers insights into fostering an environment where achievements and milestones are celebrated as a team.

The Power of Shared Celebrations

Celebrating each other's successes isn't just about the achievement itself; it's about the shared experience of joy, pride, and unity. This section explores the importance of shared celebrations in building a partnership that thrives on mutual encouragement and positivity. By celebrating together, partners can deepen their emotional connection and create lasting memories.

Acknowledging Achievements

Acknowledging achievements involves more than just a passing compliment; it's about recognizing the effort, dedication, and growth that went into reaching a milestone. This chapter discusses strategies for showing genuine appreciation for each other's accomplishments. Partners can offer words of affirmation, express enthusiasm, and celebrate the small victories that contribute to their shared journey.

Supporting Ambitions and Goals

A balanced partnership involves actively supporting each other's ambitions and goals. This section delves into the significance of being each other's biggest cheerleaders. Partners can encourage each other to pursue dreams, overcome challenges, and embrace opportunities for growth. By fostering an environment of unwavering support, couples can create a partnership that propels both individuals toward success.

Creating Rituals of Celebration

Rituals of celebration provide structure and consistency to the act of acknowledging achievements. This chapter explores the importance of creating rituals, whether it's a special dinner, a heartfelt note, or a shared activity. Partners can establish traditions that mark milestones, demonstrating their commitment to being present for each other's successes.

Sharing Achievements with Others

Sharing each other's achievements with friends, family, and loved ones strengthens the sense of partnership. This section discusses the significance of celebrating achievements within a broader community. Partners can actively promote each other's successes, sharing in the happiness and pride that comes from external recognition.

Embracing Gratitude and Joy

Celebrating achievements is also an opportunity to express gratitude for each other's contributions. This chapter addresses the importance of acknowledging how each partner's successes contribute to the partnership's overall growth and happiness. By embracing gratitude and joy, couples can create an environment where accomplishments are not just personal victories but shared triumphs.

As we delve into the realm of celebrating achievements and milestones, it's clear that this practice is essential to nurturing a balanced and equal partnership. By acknowledging each other's successes, offering unwavering support, and creating a culture of celebration, couples can enrich their relationship with positivity, mutual respect, and shared joy. The forthcoming chapters will continue to provide insights and guidance to help you celebrate each other's successes and create a partnership that thrives on shared accomplishments.

12

Cultivating an Ongoing Partnership

As we near the end of this journey, it's time to reflect on the path we've traversed in forging an equal and balanced partnership. This chapter serves as a culmination of the insights, strategies, and values that have been explored throughout the book. It summarizes key takeaways and offers guidance for maintaining a relationship that continues to thrive on collaboration, mutual growth, and shared fulfillment.

Reflecting on the Journey

The journey of creating an equal partnership is marked by a series of transformative moments. From establishing shared values to navigating conflicts, each step has contributed to the growth of the partnership. This section encourages partners to reflect on the progress made, the challenges overcome, and the victories achieved along the way. By acknowledging the journey, couples can find inspiration and motivation to continue nurturing their relationship.

Key Takeaways

Throughout the chapters, certain themes have emerged as essential to a balanced partnership:

1. Equality and Respect: Valuing each other's contributions, opinions, and aspirations forms the foundation of a balanced partnership.

2. Communication: Effective and empathetic communication is pivotal in understanding each other, resolving conflicts, and maintaining emotional connection.

3. Shared Responsibilities: Collaboratively managing household, parenting, and financial responsibilities promotes a sense of unity and equality.

4. Individuality: Respecting and supporting each other's individual needs, goals, and interests is crucial for personal growth and a strong partnership.

5. Celebration and Support: Celebrating successes, providing emotional support, and actively participating in each other's achievements reinforce mutual encouragement and joy.

Guidance for the Future

As you continue to cultivate your partnership, keep these principles in mind:

1. Continuous Growth: A partnership is a journey of ongoing growth. Embrace change, adapt to new circumstances, and consistently work together to keep the relationship flourishing.

2. Open Communication: Maintain open lines of communication. Regularly check in with each other, discuss goals, and address any concerns that arise.

3. Quality Time: Prioritize quality time together. Whether through shared experiences, date nights, or simple moments of connection, invest in

nurturing your emotional bond.

4. Flexibility: Life is full of unexpected twists. Be flexible in adapting to challenges and changes, and face them as a team.

5. Appreciation: Continue to appreciate each other's efforts, even in the smallest of gestures. Express gratitude for the partnership you've built together.

6. Seeking Help: If needed, don't hesitate to seek professional help for any challenges you encounter. Therapists, counselors, or relationship experts can provide valuable guidance.

Conclusion

The journey of forging an equal partnership is an ongoing one, marked by shared experiences, challenges, and growth. By reflecting on the lessons learned and carrying forward the principles explored in this book, you can create a partnership that thrives on collaboration, mutual support, and enduring love. As you continue on this journey, may your partnership be a beacon of equality, understanding, and shared happiness.

www.ingramcontent.com/pod-product-compliance
Lightning Source LLC
LaVergne TN
LVHW020457080526
838202LV00057B/5994